Active Citizenship: Overcoming Political Apathy in Jamaica

******

Contents

******

'IveyBooks'

****

Books written by Dr. Paul W. Ivey are called 'IveyBooks'. They share the common 'signature features' of being data-rich and well-researched. This is because in writing them he rigourously deploys the 'scholarship of integration', which is the scholarly methodology that involves the acquisition, selection, distillation, synthesizing, and contextualizing of information from numerous credible sources to create new insights and understandings for readers. It is this robust methodology that gives rise to the value proposition of 'IveyBooks': the guarantee that they will enhance readers' minds.

****

Other Books 'IveyBooks'

"I pour a lot of intellectual energy into my books ... 'IveyBooks' are well-researched and data-rich ... and the ideas and thoughts are communicated clearly with lively and lovely prose." ~ Paul W. Ivey

----

1. JAMAICA: Paradise and Paradox, Volume 1

2. JAMAICA: Paradise and Paradox, Volume 2

3. JAMAICA: Paradise and Paradox, Volume 3

4. It All Began With The May Rains: An Introvert's Remarkable Journey (Autobiography)

5. My Daughter and Me: Parenting a Polymath

6. Silent River

7. The Matriarch: The Life & Legacy of Edith "Pearl' Ivey

8. The Golden Boy

9. Toxic Masculinity: Disordered Models of Manhood in Jamaica

10. My Life Has Gone To The Dogs

****

The Case for Active & Engaged Citizens

"Eternal vigilance is the price of liberty." – *Thomas Jefferson*

My fellow Jamaican, the need for us to become active and engaged citizens is impatient of debate, especially at this time when our beloved country is experiencing a warrant of significant social and economic problems that are retarding its development and robbing many persons of the opportunity to realize their potential and become the best version of themselves.

Despite achieving some notable successes since attaining political independence from then-colonial master Britain in 1962 our country's dominant portrait now is that of a traumatized nation hobbled by many acute and chronic problems. The social infrastructure is in tatters, the economy continues to register anaemic growth, and an intractable and out-of-control full-spectrum crime situation has resulted in our beloved country having one of the highest murder rates in the world.

As citizens of Jamaica, we must never neglect, devalue, or underestimate the importance of collective expression. We must also appreciate the tremendous value of dissent in resisting majoritarian understandings of what constitutes the 'common good.' Besides, there is a saying that, "Until you are heard, you are still being too quiet."

Adult Suffrage

Jamaica achieved adult suffrage in 1944. This was a significant milestone in the country's history, as it marked the expansion of voting rights to include all adult citizens, regardless of race or gender.

Before this, voting rights were restricted based on property ownership and other criteria, disenfranchising a significant portion of the population. The attainment of adult suffrage in Jamaica was a crucial step towards creating a more inclusive and democratic society.

My fellow Jamaican, it is important for you to understand that getting the right to vote in Jamaica did not come easy.

The lead-up to adult suffrage in Jamaica was marked by a series of social, political, and economic developments. Here's a summary:

1. *Colonial Background*: Jamaica, like many other Caribbean islands, was under British colonial rule for centuries. During this time, political power was concentrated in the hands of the British colonial administrators and local elites, predominantly wealthy landowners.

2. *Emergence of Social Movements*: In the early 20th century, social movements began to emerge in Jamaica advocating for greater rights and representation for the

majority of the population, which consisted mainly of black Jamaicans and people of mixed race. These movements highlighted issues of racial discrimination, economic inequality, and lack of political representation.

3. *Labor Unrest and Civil Discontent*: The 1930s witnessed significant labor unrest and civil discontent in Jamaica, fueled by economic hardships and social injustices. Workers, particularly those in the sugar industry, organized strikes and protests demanding better wages, working conditions, and political reforms.

4. *Formation of Political Parties*: As political consciousness grew, political parties advocating for

greater autonomy and democratic reforms began to form. The Jamaican Labour Party (JLP) and the People's National Party (PNP) emerged as the two major political forces, with differing ideologies but a shared goal of achieving greater self-governance.

5. *Constitutional Reforms*: Responding to increasing pressure from Jamaicans for reform, the British colonial government introduced some constitutional changes, granting limited forms of representative government. However, these reforms fell short of meeting the demands of the burgeoning nationalist movement.

6. *Universal Adult Suffrage*: The culmination of these efforts came with the introduction of universal adult suffrage in 1944. This landmark reform granted all Jamaican citizens, regardless of race, gender, or property ownership, the right to vote in general elections. It marked a significant step towards democratic governance and paved the way for Jamaica's eventual independence from British colonial rule in 1962.

Overall, the lead-up to adult suffrage in Jamaica was characterized by grassroots activism, political mobilization, and a growing demand for social justice and equality among its diverse population.

'Citizen' Defined

But before I go any further, I think it is important for me to define 'citizen' and 'citizenship.' According to *Wikipedia*, "Citizen is the status of a person recognized under the custom or law as being a legal member of a sovereign state or belonging to a nation. (And) the idea of citizenship has been defined as the capacity of individuals to defend their rights in front of the governmental authority." And also hold their government accountable.

Being an active citizen is one of the facets of an individual **citizen's agency.**

Agency is "the degree to which an individual can make decisions about their life. To have agency means to have control over your life and the decisions that you make" [Source: Psychology Dictionary].

Being an active citizen is one of the facets of an individual **citizen's duties** as a member of the body politic.

A duty is an obligation to fulfill a specific role, responsibility, or task.

Being an active citizen is one of the facets of an individual **citizen's responsibilities** as a member of the body politic.

So, what does active and engaged citizenship 'look' like in practice? Well, to be an engaged citizen is an attitude, an ethos (a prevailing disposition), a conscious cognitive 'setting.' Therefore, to be an engaged citizen one's 'civic antenna' is always set at the "on" position enabling one to be able to perceive, process, comment, and act (as appropriate) on matters of national interest.

The Vote is Powerful

Adult suffrage refers to the right of all adult citizens to vote in elections, without any discrimination based on race, gender, property ownership, or any other criteria. It is a fundamental principle of democracy that ensures the participation of all eligible citizens in the electoral process.

Voting is crucial in a democracy as it empowers citizens to participate in governance, ensuring their voices are heard and rights upheld. Through voting, individuals shape the direction of their nation, influencing policies, laws, and leadership.

Voting also promotes accountability among elected officials, holding them responsible for fulfilling promises made during campaigns.

Additionally, voting fosters inclusivity and representation, reflecting the diversity of society in decision-making processes. It honors the sacrifices made for democratic freedoms and safeguards against tyranny.

Ultimately, voting is not just a right but a civic duty, pivotal for the preservation and advancement of democratic ideals and societal progress.

Political Apathy: A Civic Disease

But what exactly is 'voter apathy'?

In democratic societies, elections are regarded as a sanctioning or rewarding device for inducing (causing) elected officials to act in the best interest of the people, writ large. The vote is at the core of the electoral process – it is the primary thing citizens can use to hold their elected officials accountable. In other words, in the hands of citizens, the vote is a powerful instrument.

But like all other instruments, the vote is useless if it is not used. So, if many citizens do not participate in elections, elected officials will not be incentivized (encouraged) to act in their best interest. Apathy, then, presents as an absence of interest, enthusiasm, or concern among voters that translates into a low 'turnout' for elections.

Governments must fear their people.

But the unfortunate consequence of apathy is that it incentivizes politicians to act with impunity (recklessness) because they do not fear the wrath of citizens.

And as a corollary to the foregoing, citizens must also fear their governments becoming intoxicated by the allure of power and becoming authoritarian or acting in a manner that favours only narrow special interests and not the majority of the people.

This fear of their governments 'going rogue' must be a central motivating force for active and engaged citizenship! Note well, my fellow Jamaican.

So, how is 'voter apathy' measured? The percentage of votes cast on Election Day in relation to the number of eligible voters is termed the 'voter turnout' and it is a proxy measure for 'voter apathy.' Yes, voter turnout is an important indicator of how citizens participate in the governance of their country. Higher voter turnout is taken as a gauge of the vitality of democracy, whereas lower turnout is regarded as voter apathy and mistrust of the political process. Fierce and calcified (hardened) voter apathy is considered to be one of the main causes of low voter turnout [Source: The Electoral Commission of Jamaica, Terms of Reference for Research Project on Voter Apathy in Jamaica].

The view has been expressed that, "(Jamaica's) electoral majority is frustrated by two political dinosaurs (the JLP and PNP) determined to keep Jamaica enslaved to a colonial culture of political patronage, corruption, and cronyism" [Source: Gordon Robinson, Attorney-at-Law, The Gleaner, December 17, 2019].

What, then, is the actual level of voter apathy in Jamaica?

The failure of successive political administrations (JLP and PNP) over the past six decades to make life better for most Jamaicans, and their impotence in dealing with social problems (especially crime), have severely eroded public confidence in these political parties.

Put another way, a large swath of the Jamaican population is apathetic to the political process and also harbours antipathy and outright resentment for politicians.

In 2017 on the occasion of Jamaica's 55th anniversary as an Independent country, a poll commissioned by The Gleaner newspaper found that 49 percent of respondents were of the view Jamaica would have fared better officially remaining a colony of Britain.

The results of the poll represent the deep disappointment many Jamaicans feel about the shambolic manner in which their country has been governed since Independence, by the two political parties that have alternated in governing the country.

In addition, one of the most noteworthy things about the 2016 General Election was that, at just 47.72 %, the voter turnout was the lowest in Jamaica's history, since Universal Adult Suffrage in 1944 ('suffrage' is the right to vote in political elections). The only time voter turnout was lower than in 2016 was the uncontested General Election in 1983 that was boycotted by the PNP – the voter turnout then was 15%.

The victorious party in the 2016 election, the JLP, won 436,972 votes or 23.95% of the 1,824,410 voters on the voters' list. In other words, the party that came into power (the JLP) won less than 25% of the available votes; and the Opposition (the PNP) garnered 433,735 votes or 23.77% of the available votes [Source: The Electoral Commission of Jamaica].

So, reflecting pervasive (widespread) apathy, more than 50% of the electorate did not vote in the 2016 General Election! They want different. Such is the level of disillusionment with Jamaica's brand of decadent and putrid politics.

Yes, there is something repellant about the nature of Jamaican politics such that it is unable to attract more of the younger people in the population, whether as new voters or as participants in the political process.

I will now share an example of the 'mindset' of a young, apathetic Jamaican citizen. I'm not sure if the passage of time has caused him to change his mind, but, in an article in *The Gleaner* on June 15, 2001, titled "Why I Refuse to Vote," Melville Cooke curated several reasons why he was disgusted with the Jamaican brand of 'dutty politics' and would have absolutely nothing to do with it. In a similar fashion to Pontius Pilate, the fifth governor of the Roman province of

Judaea, who wanted nothing to do with Jesus' crucifixion, Melville Cooke has 'washed his hands' of Jamaica's 'dutty politics.'

This is what Cooke passionately wrote: "I, Mel Cooke, being of sound mind and of my own free will, refuse to be enumerated, much less vote. I have never held a National Identification Card and the only ink that has ever been on my fingers is from a faulty ball-point pen. My earliest recollection of political activity is parts of the 1980 election campaign. Then 9 years old, I saw an aspiring Member of Parliament handing out Cheese-Trix in Morant Bay. I don't know if I was more disgusted by the donor or the recipients – and there were many. It was also a time when I first heard a gunshot fired in anger, as a motorcade passed on the main road, and we later learnt that someone's finger had been shot off."

Melville Cooke did not stop at this juncture; oh no, he ploughed on, propelled by palpable disgust: "Both parties have failed to reach an acceptable standard in shaping Jamaica. Choosing between the JLP and the PNP is about the same as being cornered by two thieves. One says he or she is going to rob then kill you, the other says he or she will kill then rob you and you need to pick an option. Not much choice, is there? And I can never forget that it is really a matter of life or death. Not one political heavyweight has ever had to flee their home under police guard. Not one of them has ever been the victim of a drive-by shooting. Not one of them has had their home fire-bombed. Basic life amenities are a right, not a privilege as the JLP and PNP would have us believe. [Besides], we will never know how so many people have died, and lives destroyed in pursuit of political power in Jamaica."

And then Mel Cooke delivered his scathing 'verdict': "I cannot stop political bigwigs from honouring dead thugs with their prominent presence at their funerals. I cannot stop large contracts from being awarded to party faithfuls. I cannot hold anyone responsible for the missing money which the Auditor General reports every year without fail. But I can refuse to vote. And I do. I know it does not stop either party one bit. I know their faithful fools will continue to vote and fight for them and one leader or the other will claim to have "the people's mandate." But in this crazy, nasty, unfair, deadly thing we call Jamaican politics it is the one choice I am able to make. And I find it enormously satisfying."

To be sure, Melville Cooke's dissertation is quite an indictment of Jamaica's putrid and emetogenic brand of politics that he was exposed to at a tender age. And he is clearly traumatized by it. And he is not alone.

But when citizens disengage from the political process, their action amounts to feckless abdication (rejection) and abandonment of the key duties and responsibilities appertaining (connected) to their 'office'! Such gross dereliction (forsaking) of duty amounts to 'civic negligence.'

The non-engagement by citizens animated, frustrated, and pained Keith Anthony 'Tony' Laing, a musicologist and cultural activist, prompting him to passionately and repeatedly say (when he hosted a talk show on Power 106 FM Radio Station): "Jamaica is like a company and the citizens are the shareholders, but wi lef it up, wi lef it up enuh .... and that's why the company name Jamaica is in the terrible condition it is in today."

What is more, Tony Laing said what he said many years ago, but sadly, **my fellow Jamaican**, we continue to "lef up" Jamaica to feckless politicians, heartless criminals, ne'er-do-wells, and others of similar nefarious dispositions.

And in an article in *The Daily Observer* newspaper of August 14, 2019, titled 'As a Nation, We Are at Fault,' writer and educator Romane Elliston declared: "As a people, we are hypocrites, we turn a blind eye to injustice, we protect criminals and thugs (the Government included) and then we lie in wait for a hero, a saviour. But I say, up, up you mighty race! None but ourselves can liberate our nation. Too many of us are afraid to die. But I tell you, when we no longer fear death, then the enemy has no power over us. Our forefathers did not let the fear of death cripple them. They fought and won although they died, but we tasted freedom by their sacrifice. Stand up for your children and their children's children. Stand up for the rich heritage fought and earned by our forefathers. My people, we do not require dragon slayers nor superhuman beings, but a people who know fear, admit their fear but are ready just the same to fight. Let us rid ourselves of our failed and corrupt government. Enough is enough! We cannot afford for our beautiful nation to sink any further."

Sadly, though, Jamaica *continues* to 'sink further.'

Attorney-at-Law Leighton Miller puts the responsibility for the 'condition Jamaica is in,' and the fact that Jamaica is 'sinking further,' squarely at the feet of his fellow Jamaicans.

In a Facebook post on October 02, 2019, Miller was characteristically and unapologetically blunt when he wrote: "The problem is not the politicians. It is you. All who support them. Looking for bly, favours, contracts, jobs, etc. All who run up enna dem picture and drop dem name … and mek sure sey foonu pickney and fi dem pickney a friend. Oonu a di problem. Nuh, dem!"

Clearly, then, Jamaicans must change for better for Jamaica to change for better.

Sadly, Laing, Elliston, and Miller are right.

Active, hypervigilant, fearless, responsible, and engaged citizens are the *sine qua non* (an essential condition or necessary thing) for the proper functioning of a democratic society, which Jamaica is.

On the other hand, jaywalking, cognitively anesthetized, feckless, or lobotomized citizens are bad for Jamaica.

The first type of citizens will keep a government honest, but the second type lets it run amok with the affairs of the country. Indeed, democracy stems from the *Greek* word '*demokratia*' which means 'rule by people.'

Alas, though, faced with the unappealing binary choice of either the Jamaica Labour Party (JLP) or the People's National Party (PNP), the 'civic disease' of political apathy (see definition below) has taken root and is spreading among the Jamaican citizenry. Already, a large swath of the population is afflicted.

Sociologist Peter Espeut puts it this way: "Those of us Jamaicans with sensitive consciences find it difficult to be identified with political parties chronically implicated in corruption or that maintain political garrisons, or which refuse to disassociate themselves from political thugs and armed enforcers. This could explain why the number of Jamaicans who vote for both major political parties has steadily declined in recent years because they both fall into the categories outlined above. I expect another low turnout in the next general election unless one party or the other promises to take credible steps against political corruption" ['Jamaicans Have Sensitive Consciences, *The Gleaner*, January 17, 2020].

But democracy declines or dies from a distracted, feckless, 'unwoke', indifferent, jaywalking, cognitively anesthetized, or lobotomized citizenry.

Therefore, **my fellow Jamaican**, if we allow ourselves to be consumed by apathy, we betray the sacrifices our ancestors made fighting for the freedoms and rights we now enjoy and routinely take for granted. However, in the African tradition, betraying one's ancestors is to invite ill fortune and failure in life.

So, however slow, however incomplete, however challenged we are, we must never as citizens tune out and lose interest in the affairs of our country because we can indeed create the change that we desire.

But we must have the appetency (desire).

The tragedy is that we deny ourselves possibilities when we lose hope and instead entertain hopelessness. Alas, apathy evinces hopelessness.

Toward Active Citizenship!

****

Cures for Political Apathy

****

So, how might the 'civic disease' called apathy be cured?

No More '9-Day Wonders'

Writing in *The Gleaner* on June 30, 2023, free-thinking public affairs opinionator Kristen Gyles mentioned that "Here in Jamaica, everything is pejoratively dubbed a 'nine-day wonder'. The truth is, there is nothing profound or strange about public discourse on a particular subject dying down with the passage of time. Obviously, an emotionally stirring report of any injustice will cause an immediate uproar which will not last forever. But rather than critiquing the length of time it takes people to get back to regular programming each and every time there is injustice, why not focus on why it is that our nine days of complaining and bellyaching seem to so often yield no fruit? Could it be that we spend our valuable nine days bickering with each other over the chosen means of protest? Could it be that the few protests that are organised are poorly supported? A big part of the reason that nine days comes and goes with no change sometimes is because our strength lies in our unity and it seems we have very little. Take, for example, the recent study conducted by the Brattle Group, which quantified the reparations due to Jamaica arising from the Transatlantic Chattel Slavery as being many trillions of dollars. Jamaicans have got more excited over the opening of a new doughnut shop. Over the years, several conversations have been had regarding the need for reparations but if the conversations are largely being held by a minority of people with little collective interest having been garnered, who will pay Jamaica a cent? We have to start linking our collective advocacy to the progress we make as a country. Nothing tried, nothing gained. There is power in unity, in advocacy, and in standing together. If we all do the 'little' that lies within our power, we can actually make the nine days count."

Reject the Status Quo!

More. Writing in the *The Daily Observer* newspaper on September 18, 2019, Dr. Raulston Nembhard, a priest and social commentator, 'wrote the following prescription' as a cure for apathy: "So, where do we stand? What are the growing numbers of Jamaicans who have grown disheartened with the political process to do? Well, we can accept the *status quo* as given or as something that we cannot change. We can continue to sit on the fence or whine on our social media platforms. Or we can get engaged and organise to effect the change that we desire. The latter option seems to me to be the best one. We all have a sense of what can be achieved when the enormous power of social media is harnessed and put to work for a good cause. But that cause has to have an agenda, a core set of principles that people can buy into. It must be motivated by a love for country and the urgent need to see change that can benefit the greater Jamaica. I would suggest that an essential aspect of this agenda must be constitutional reform with a view of a new paradigm of governance."

Shared Ownership

Also, in a speech on July 15, 2019, Richard Pandohie, President of the Jamaica Manufacturers and Exporters Association (JMEA), hit the nail squarely on the head when he averred that: "Jamaica is our shared enterprise; we will have to accept that Jamaica is our business, whether you're a manufacturer, exporter, entertainer, hotelier or farmer, Jamaica is where we have all planted our roots, made significant investment and are raising our families."

Pandohie was echoing the overarching goal of Vision 2030, Jamaica's national development plan, which is: "Jamaica, the place of choice to live, work, do business, and raise families."

The Role of Intellectuals

Society needs its intellectuals, thought leaders and opinion shapers to help the populace understand important matters. And one very important matter concerns the duties and responsibilities of a citizen in a democratic society.

To avoid redundancy, intellectuals must engage society practically, vocationally, and through activism.

Noam Chomsky sets out three responsibilities of intellectuals in his now classic paper, 'The Responsibility of Intellectuals': to speak the truth and expose lies; to provide historical context; and to lift the veil of ideology, the underlying framework of ideas that limits the boundaries of debate." This is, or should be, truistic.

It's just obvious that intellectuals should tell the truth. It is equally obvious that it is not only intellectuals who have this responsibility. Noam Chomsky argues that, in a society, intellectuals have responsibilities that go beyond the responsibilities of others because they have a particularly privileged position.

The combination of training, facilities, political liberty, access to information, and freedom of expression enjoyed by some intellectuals imposes deeper responsibilities on them.

Another reason that we need reminding of the truisms in Chomsky's essay is that, in the face of the temptation not to make a fuss, not to rock the boat, and not to endanger one's livelihood, it is almost always easier to serve the interests of the powerful, or to say and do nothing, than it is to stand up for what is right by speaking out." [Source: 'The Responsibility of Intellectuals: Reflections by Noam Chomsky and others after 50 years,' 2019, edited by Nicholas Allott, Chris Knight and Neil Smith]

Interestingly, Noam Chomsky made a distinction between 'value-oriented', 'technocratic-oriented,' and 'policy-oriented' intellectuals.

In this typology of intellectuals, 'technocratic and policy-oriented intellectuals' are the 'good guys', in the eyes of the establishment, who merely serve external power whereas the 'value-oriented intellectuals' (the 'bad guys', from an establishment perspective) are those who engage in critical analysis (of history, the status quo, and policy proposals) because they have a 'moral responsibility as decent human beings … to advance the causes of freedom, justice, mercy, peace … [as opposed to] … the role they are expected to play, serving … leadership and established institutions.

But happily, and thankfully, Martin Henry, who was a Gleaner newspaper Columnist, Philosopher, Polymath, Public Intellectual, and a quintessential Active Citizen, did this most admirably for three decades!

So, concerning the duties and responsibilities of the citizen, in a column published in *The Sunday Gleaner* of April 14, 2019, Martin

Henry dutifully reminded us, his **fellow Jamaicans**, that:

"Voting is only one element of a citizen's political engagement in a democracy. And it may not even be the most important one. The politically rich and original notion of 'citizen' is one who is actively engaged in the life of a political community (the polity) with a set of rights, responsibilities, and duties, and who understands the political and economic processes, institutions, laws, rights, and responsibilities of the polity. [Besides] that citizen is himself/herself a potential candidate for participation in the governance of the polity to which he/she belongs."

But Martin Henry didn't stop here. He went on to enumerate some of the ways, as **Jamaicans**, we've 'lef tings up' – that is, neglected our duties and responsibilities as citizens:

1. "We, the citizens, can and should take other actions in the discharge of our responsibilities, with or without voting. The Green Papers of the Parliament allow citizens' input into the formulation of law and policy. Very few make submissions written or oral. Anyone can request to appear before a Joint Select Committee of Parliament to argue a position.

2. We don't pressure our constituency representatives to represent our interests in the Parliament. They can bank on our somnolence and they represent their party's interests. We don't form enough groups to agitate for change. Versed in the art of scrounging for personal favours, we don't lobby ministers in the larger public interest.

3. We don't use media with strategic dexterity to orchestrate public pressure on Government. And media, the Fourth Estate, does not probe deeply and consistently the shortcomings and corruption of Government.

4. We don't make recommendations to public agencies to give feedback to the political directorate for change.
5. We vote – in declining numbers – and go back to sleep. And it suits the Government."

As so cogently articulated by Martin Henry, in a democracy, certain duties and responsibilities (obligations) are part and parcel of the 'office of citizen' that go beyond merely voting periodically.

An active and engaged citizenry is a critical element in the design and proper functioning of a democracy.

In other words, a democracy devoid of engaged and active citizens is dysfunctional. Citizens, therefore, must not be apathetic.

Reiterating. If citizens choose to be apathetic, such a stance is tantamount to 'civic negligence' or 'civic jaywalking'– the abdication of the duties and responsibilities of their 'office.'

This is a serious threat to democracy!

I am aware that, for this reason, the Electoral Commission of Jamaica is embarking on a study "to provide a factual and evidence-based understanding of participation in elections and governance in Jamaica with the aim of clarifying the gaps to be filled or opportunities to be harnessed to increase, both quantitatively and qualitatively, the meaningful participation in elections and governance" [Source: The Electoral Commission of Jamaica, Terms of Reference for Research Project on Voter Apathy in Jamaica].

"A State cannot govern itself. It finds expression and executes its functions through individuals; hence the State is human. Its animation reflects a nation's human characters." [Source: Marcus Garvey, The Philosophy and Opinions]

It is citizens who make democracy work! Active citizens!

Engaged citizens!

However, the actions Martin Henry enumerated above that many of my fellow Jamaicans are

not doing as citizens, are *exactly* the actions we should be doing!

Like Martin Henry, whose sudden passing on May 28, 2019, left a huge void in the 'ideas and public dialogue marketplace' in Jamaica, I am calling on you, **my fellow Jamaican**, to become an active and engaged citizen!

Starting now!

So, even if Melville Cooke and others like him maintain their stance of not voting, there are many other ways they can discharge their obligations as citizens.

Because the future belongs to them, and the present will determine the nature of the future, I am calling on the Jamaican youths, especially, to become actively engaged in the affairs of their country.

The Jamaican population is relatively young, with a median age of 29.4 years.

Jamaica's future belongs to its young people. And they should resent what has been done, and continues to be done, that will impair their prospects of having a bright future in their own country.

Youthfulness in and of itself is a great power. Indeed, the Bible says the youths are called upon because they are strong.

Samantha Power, a former aide to 44th US President Obama, told Yale University's graduating class of 2016: "Know that history is not in a hurry but that you can help speed it up."

En passant (in passing) I must say Martin Henry's sudden demise calls into question the Epicurean philosophy that death is harmless. How can this be when death cuts short plans, projects, and responsibilities while plunging family and friends of deceased persons into grief?

You know, several years ago, journalist and environmental activist John Maxwell averred that: "For me, the real failure of democracy in Jamaica is in the failure of public dialogue." Alas, Maxwell is correct, because the quality of public dialogue in Jamaica is indeed poor — shallow and polluted and poisoned by partisan political drivel (nonsense).

And it is in this regard that Martin Henry's incessant advocacy and cognitively rich contributions proved immensely valuable. And will be sorely missed. But, thankfully, he has bequeathed (left) to us and future generations a rich legacy of his ideas through his written commentaries.

I consider it a privilege to have been Martin Henry's work colleague for nine years and to have had the opportunity to engage in frequent discussions with him about matters of national interest.

He has inspired me.

I once asked Martin how he was able to sustain writing his *Gleaner* newspaper column for 30 years despite not seeing immediate results of his advocacy for change. His response was a gem. He responded that, when breaking rocks, it's not the last blow that shatters them, but the cumulative effect of all the previous blows.

Calling Out Young Jamaicans

Commenting on the perceived apathy among Jamaica's millennials ('Generation Y' or the 'Net Generation' - persons born between 1981 to 1996), Kelly McIntosh in an article in *The Gleaner* on September 28, 2016, noted that, "Our millennials are products of Jamaica. What they are today is informed by what they have seen around them for several years now.

Their apparent apathy is possibly simply a rejection of our preoccupation as a nation with form and appearance at the expense of real substance. Jamaica reached where we are under our watch. Why do we, therefore, expect our young people to rise up and push back now? They are simply modelling our own behaviour. Do all Jamaican citizens have an equal voice? Is enforcement of the law predictable? Are our authorities seen to be fair? To answer any of these questions in the negative is to support the argument that the State lacks legitimacy. Our young people will continue to demonstrate this so-called apathy, being true to our own example in allowing governance lacking legitimacy."

Neil Howe and William Strauss, authors of the 1991 book *'Generations: The History of America's Future, 1584 to 2069,'* are often credited with coining the term. Millennials are the last generation born in the 20th century, and this year (2020) they are between 24-38 years old. So, with a median age of 29.4 years, the Jamaican population is comprised mostly of Millennials.

For the sake of Jamaica, I hope *Kelly McIntosh* is wrong and Jamaica's Millennials will be motivated by their individual and collective self-interest to become active citizens.

Also worthy of note concerning the dispositions of Jamaica's young people is a 2018 study - *'Teens and Technology: Young Jamaicans in a*

Hyper-Connected World' - led by Professor Paul Golding of the University of Technology, Jamaica. The study revealed that the main online activities of Jamaican teens ('Generation Z') were communication and entertainment, but the use of technology for creative uses and civic engagement was extremely low. 'Generation Z' is the demographic cohort that succeeded Millennials ('Generation Y') and was born between 1995-2015.

"The results involving civic engagements were not encouraging. For example, 65% of students have never posted comments on a news site and 44% have never sent links of news stories or information about current events. This finding suggests that there is continued work to be done to help young Jamaicans become more civically engaged online."

Jamaica's young people have been militant in the past. On October 15, 1968, the Government of Jamaica, with Hugh Shearer as Prime Minister, declared Guyanese historian, political activist, and academic Walter Rodney *persona non grata* (an unacceptable or unwelcome person).

The decision to ban Rodney led to protests among students at the University of the West Indies, Mona Campus, and wider, to include large sections of the working class communities. Jamaican university youths were 'militant' at the time! It was a kind of *'youth aroused'* situation that, sadly, has waned over the years.

However, I observed what I regarded as a glimmer of hope on February 20, 2019, when *students* of the University of Technology, Jamaica (UTech, Jamaica) *joined* with staff members to *protest* the comparatively low level of financial support that was being allocated to the institution by the Government of Jamaica.

I regarded the action of the UTech, Jamaica students, in joining the protest, as a positive sign that they were not lobotomized and could indeed be roused into taking action. I was heartened by the students' action because I was sorely disappointed when they did not protest the murder of their fellow student Shanique Walters on November 4, 2015, to send a message to the government, to implement effective and sustained crime prevention and control strategies.

Jamaica's future belongs to its young people and they should resent what has been done and continues to be done now to Jamaica that will impair their prospects of having a bright future.

Therefore, I would welcome the day when Jamaica's young people, especially those in tertiary institutions (because that's where future leaders are most likely to emerge), again begin to take a greater interest in matters of national concern, particularly crime and corruption.

Greta Thunberg, who was named *Time Magazine's* 'Person of the Year' for 2019, and who was also a nominee for the Nobel Peace Prize, is a 16-year-old Swedish environmental activist, who has been courageously 'calling out' world leaders to take bold and decisive action on climate change.

Cataloguing feedback to its naming of Thunberg 'Person of the Year' for 2019, *Time Magazine* quoted a reader as saying, Thunberg "inspired her on her own journey to being a climate-change activist."

Another reader, a local government representative, said "When I see my younger constituents becoming more engaged in community affairs, I give Thunberg credit for the change." And another reader averred that *Thunberg* proves the old saying that "one person can make a difference."

But dare we entertain hope for the emergence of a Jamaican Millennial or GenXer, who, like the courageous Thunberg, or the militant Peter Tosh, will 'call out' our politicians into raising the bar on governance, starting with reining in corruption, and wanton public disorder and lawlessness? Dare we hope?

Perhaps rather than simply hoping, we the 'elders' should set a better example for them, and also actively cheer on our young people. Interestingly, there is a Youth Parliament in Jamaica, but it is more form than substance.

Cauterise Political Cultists

In addition to 'civic negligence' (i.e., apathy), also bad for democracy are political sycophants, who indulge their political biases without reason or restraint. These motivated sycophants will blindly defend anything the political party they support does no matter how bad the action is and will condemn everything the political party they do not support does, no matter how good the action is.

The hardcore base of the JLP and the PNP is made up of many

political sycophants who display all the classical signs of being cultists.

A friend of mine, *Vincent Gordon*, avers that there are three dominant national identities in Jamaica: (1) 'Jamaican'; (2) 'PNP' (supporter); and (3) 'JLP' supporter. This tripartite national identity may seem funny, but it is not far from the truth.

Citizenship Education & More

In February 2019, the US-based Aspen Institute in collaboration with the John S. and James L. Knight Foundation released a report on *'Trust, Media, and Transparency.'* Asserting that "democracy and the news are inextricably intertwined," and concluding that "it is clear that both are in crisis," the report contained specific recommendations to restore trust in media and democracy.

With specific reference to citizenship, the above-mentioned report noted that: "Citizens need knowledge as well as the opportunity and a sense of responsibility to participate fully in public debate and other democratic activities. Every citizen should have a basic understanding of the Constitution."

The report continued, "Citizens also need opportunities to engage in productive dialogue about local civic matters with others who hold opposing political viewpoints." In addition, the said report went even further and recommended the following specific actions to engender engaged citizenship:

1. "Provide students of all ages with basic civic education.

2. Reach across the political divide. Communities should develop programs hosted by trusted local institutions to facilitate dialogue among citizens. These exchanges should address important questions ranging from local issues to relevant constitutional questions. Public libraries are one obvious place for such discussions. Also, public awareness campaigns should be developed to encourage people to participate in civic institutions.

3. Encourage commitment to a year of national service. As politics

has become increasingly tribalised, citizens have lost a shared sense of citizenship. To address this, the time has come to revitalize efforts to encourage a year of voluntary national service to help renew trust in democratic institutions."

In my view, the recommended actions mentioned immediately above are relevant to Jamaica and should be either adapted and/or adopted.

Activism: Examples & Testimonials

In the summer of 2001, as part of a master's degree in Adult Education/Lifelong Learning I was pursuing with Mount St. Vincent University, located in Halifax

Canada, one of the courses was a 'Summer Institute' in that country.

The residential Summer Institute was titled **'Active Citizenship'** and it was held at the Coast Guard College, Sydney, Nova Scotia.

One of the highlights of the Institute was a panel discussion by persons who were already active citizens.

These persons shared what triggered them – what got them off their butts, so to speak. In each instance, bar none, they wanted an existing situation in 'their space' to *change*, so they directed their rage purposefully to become catalysts for the change they wished to see.

The ardent appetence (desire) of the panelists was palpable and instructive and reminded me of how *Marcus Garvey* – Jamaica's first National Hero - was *stirred into action* by the awful conditions facing African Jamaicans in early post-Emancipation Jamaica.

Also, as *Barack Obama* famously proclaimed on February 5, 2008, "Change will not come if we wait for some other person or some other time. We are the ones we've been waiting for. We are the change that we seek!"

In addition, "go out and vote!" was *Obama's* advice to Blacks and other Americans distressed by the odious Trumpism (reflected in the resurgence of white supremacy) that has reared its ugly head in America with the election of one *Donald Trump* as President, in 2016.

Another contemporary example of an active citizen, who could have simply sat back and enjoyed her cushy life, is Guyanese-British businesswoman and author *Gina Miller*, who, spending her own money, initiated court action against the British government over its authority to withdraw from the European Union (Brexit) without approval from Parliament.

In an interview with Stephen Sackur on his hard-hitting BBC television programme *HardTalk*, Miller said she was motivated to act by the desire to ensure that the sovereignty of Parliament and adherence to the rule of law were not tramped on.

Her court case was successful. She attracted incoming missiles and opprobrium and took a lot of flak, yet she persisted.

My Awakening

My attendance at, and participation in, the abovementioned Summer Institute on Active Citizenship, in Canada, stirred and awakened 'something' inside me.

That 'something' was akin to an epiphany (a sudden realization) and I became intensely enamoured of (captivated) the idea of *engaged citizenship*.

Oh yes, the Summer Institute caused me to see things differently

— it opened new cognitive vistas as catalysts for action on my part as a Jamaican citizen.

You see, *Adult Educators*, being *Intellectuals*, must be change agents by being active citizens! This is because "Adult learning is more central to societal reproduction, resistance, and transformation than that of the children. Resistance to and transformation of societal structures emerges from the adult population and is premised upon men and women's ability to learn new ways of seeing the world and acting within it." [Source: Professor Michael Welton, *Rendering the Invisible Visible*, 1987]

People Power & Reasons for Hope

Jeanette Calder (Executive Director of the Jamaica Accountability Meter Portal), *Prof. Trevor Munroe* (Founding Executive Director of the National Integrity Action), *Carol Narcisse* (of the Jamaica Civil Society Coalition), *Susan Goffe* (of Jamaicans for Justice), and others, confidently assert that there are reasons to be hopeful that determined citizen action individually, or collectively, can force elected and other non-elected officials to act in the best interest of the majority of the people and not to the advantage 'special interests' or themselves.

There are indeed examples, both internationally and in Jamaica, of citizen activism (the wielding of

#PeoplePower) that brought about change. I will now cite some real examples to support this point:

United States of America: In the USA, constituents often accost their Senators or Congressional Representatives in their offices or flood them with calls. Or 'giving it to them' at Town Hall meetings. Some of these elected officials have even been locked in their offices by determined constituents showing them who the real boss is. Given that we Jamaicans admire 'foreign things,' the above forms of **#PeoplePower** are worthy of emulation.

From Kristen Gyles: "Following the May 2020 murder of George Floyd by a police officer who kneeled on his neck, there were protests all over the world and despite the few who made it their point of duty to naysay, a global discussion was sparked not only surrounding police brutality and how it can be prevented but also around racial prejudice. That incident and the protests it sparked raised global awareness on an unprecedented level, created a platform for the ventilation of the racial issues faced by black Americans, and paved the way for legislative changes, including the banning of the police practice of using chokeholds or neck restraints and the signing of an executive order to create a federal database of fired police officers and officers with multiple instances of misconduct. Since the protests, the US has also seen the introduction of the George Floyd Justice in Policing Act of 2020 which was intended to limit the use of excessive force by police officers." [Source: The Gleaner]

Hong Kong: In Hong Kong, hundreds of thousands of determined citizens who oppose a proposed law by the government that makes provisions for the extradition of persons to mainland China have been protesting since April 2019. The basis for the protests is that the proposed law has within it the seeds that will germinate and, in the long run, undermine the country's judicial independence and put dissidents at risk. The proposed law was withdrawn by Carrie Lam, the country's leader, in September 2019, but the protesters expanded their demands to include full democracy and an inquiry into police actions. *Washington Post* columnist George F. Will on December 27, 2019, stated that "Nothing more momentous happened in 2019 than Hong Kong's heroic insurrection." **#PeoplePower!**

Lebanon: Conditions in this country were bad – high prices and poor public services were the norm. But the proverbial 'straw that broke the camel's back' was the imposition by the government of a tax on WhatsApp messages. The people erupted in mass protest and they did not let up until Prime

Minister Saad Hariri announced his resignation on October 30, 2019. **#PeoplePower!**

Some examples of **#PeoplePower** from Jamaica include the following:

Extending the Time for Releasing Cabinet Documents: On October 1, 2019, *The Gleaner* newspaper reported that "The Leader of Government Business in the Parliament (House of Representatives), Karl Samuda, moved an affirmative resolution seeking to amend the Access to Information Act, which would move the exemption (of the release of Cabinet documents) from 20 years to 70 years. The order, dated September 5, was signed by Prime

Minister Andrew Holness, who leads the Cabinet."

But the public outrage across the length and breadth of Jamaica and on social media at the temerity of the government to want to conceal the people's business from the people for an entire lifetime was swift, vociferous, and pellucidly clear: we will not have any of it! Within four days Prime Minister Holness was forced to withdraw the indecent proposal. **#PeoplePower!**

In an interview with *The Gleaner* newspaper, Professor Munroe of the anti-corruption watch-dog organization National Integrity Action (NIA) said the "U-turn (by the Government) demonstrates yet again that the voice of the people does matter (and) we hope that this experience will discourage this – or any other – Government from proposals to undermine principles of transparency and accountability."

The irony of the situation though is that Andrew Holness is the same prime minister who claims to be 'new and different' and who, at his inauguration, and repeatedly since, promised transparency in his administration. Double-Speaker-in-Chief? Or deeper character trait?

Another interesting and revealing twist to the ill-fated 'Cabinet documents saga' was the claim by Prime Minister Holness that he had secured an agreement from the Leader of the Opposition, Dr. Peter Phillips, on the matter.

The plot thickened when Dr. Phillips strenuously denied agreeing to the proposal, stating that the Prime Minister's account was: "untrue and an incomplete and unfaithful representation of the conversation between us."

In other words, Dr. Phillips was asserting the prime minister was prevaricating. And for good measure, Phillips added that the episode once again revealed a pattern where "the prime minister chooses to breach trust and standing conventions by giving his own untrue and self-serving accounts of private conversations, in an effort to show himself in a positive light" [Source: The Gleaner, October 6, 2019].

Notwithstanding the tart denial from Dr. Phillips, cynics have expressed the view that such self-serving collusion between politicians is not far-fetched. **#PeoplePower** rebuffed this attempted trespass on Jamaican citizens' right to know (RTK) what has been done in their name by politicians.

Bauxite Mining in the Cockpit Country: News that licenses were issued to a company to mine bauxite in the 'Cockpit Country' – an important ecological and historical region of northwestern Jamaica that is also home to many endemic species of plants - elicited howls of protests from citizens of the affected communities and the wider society; persons have marched on the Parliament, and societal influencers (including popular musicians, and dancehall artistes) have joined in the chorus of opposition to what will be ecocide if mining were allowed to proceed.

A group of Jamaicans in New York, USA, also demonstrated in front of the United Nations Building while the General Assembly was in session, on September 26, 2019, and while the Jamaica Prime Minister was inside speaking about, of all things, climate change.

The firm demonstration of 'People Power' concerning 'Cockpit Country' has forced the government to temporarily draw brakes, but a mighty battle is shaping up.

En passant, I would also like for public pressure to be brought on the Holness administration's insistence on 'planting concrete' and thereby undermining Jamaica's long-term food security by building 17,000 houses on the Bernard Lodge property, in St. Catherine, where some of the country's most fertile agricultural soils (Class 1) are located.

Commenting on the perennial anaemic economic growth Jamaica has experienced and how the agriculture sector might be leveraged to drive growth, Professor Densil Williams of The University of the West Indies said:

"Interestingly, instead of using the best lands for agriculture and attracting investments like the Azan-type (a prominent local businessman) model at Bernard Lodge, the Government is pushing to build houses and all sorts of non-value-added activities. Re-prioritising the Bernard Lodge lands for high value-added agriculture and seeking strong investors should be an immediate policy priority if any meaningful growth is to be derived in the short term" [Source: The Sunday, October 27, 2019].

Also, given that only about 37% of Jamaica is suitable for agriculture but just 19.5% is now available for farming, and Jamaica has a food import bill of US$900 million, building houses on the Bernard

Lodge lands is a horribly bad policy, and the only thing worse than formulating bad policy is implementing bad policy. Good policy thinking is needed.

The National Environment and Planning Agency (NEPA) is a co-conspirator of chaos in Jamaica. Well, it emerged in the Public Administration and Appropriations Committee (PAAC) of Parliament on November 6, 2019, that, over the years, having regarded the Bernard Lodge lands as among Jamaica's "most fertile soils – Class 1 soils," NEPA consistently denied developments from taking place here. However, as soon as it became the developer, on instructions from the Cabinet, a pliable NEPA approved various developments, including housing, to occur there.

Citizens must resist this Bernard Lodge travesty that will forever foreclose thousands of hectares of Jamaica's "most fertile soils" from being available for their best use - agriculture. Besides, scientists have warned that, with the reality of climate change, the yield from current agricultural lands could decline by as much as a third requiring 33% more land to produce the same amount of food. **#PeoplePower** must be deployed to stop the Bernard Lodge travesty!

Resignation of Former Prime Minister Bruce Golding: This was a first in Jamaica – a Prime Minister forced to resign in the face of insistent demands from the public, the Opposition party, and civil society after his government was rocked by the scandal resulting from a stand-off with the US Government over the extradition of drug kingpin, racketeer, and 'Don' of the JLP garrison of Tivoli Gardens. Golding has failed to do the right thing in the moment of choice.

There is indeed redemption, because Golding, now a Distinguished Fellow at the UWI, has been making useful contributions through well-researched columns in the local newspapers and speeches.

Pushback on the 'Acting CJ' Appointment – Prime Minister

Holness appointed Justice Bryan Sykes as 'acting Chief Justice (CJ)' in February 2018. This was in effect putting the CJ on probation to prove his mettle. But key stakeholders in the society were up in arms against this constitutional aberration that was unprecedented.

The PM would not budge, offering instead, a wholly unconvincing justification. The public would have none of it. Lawyers, talk radio hosts, callers, letter writers, newspaper editorial boards, and everyday people kept up the pressure until the prime minister dithered to save face but buckled and capitulated under the powerful pushback. Another instance of **#PeoplePower!**

Additional Prescriptions

The examples I've listed above show what **#PeoplePower** can do when citizens make clear to politicians who is the true boss in a democracy - the people! But such actions must be sustained; hence I'm ending this pop-up book with the following additional prescriptions:

Civic Education

Jamaica is witnessing much civic disengagement and civic negligence that is reflected in the high level of voter apathy present in society. Also, many young Jamaicans are not equipped with the skills and knowledge necessary to contribute to the political future of Jamaica as a free and democratic society.

Therefore, our educational institutions must assist in addressing the situation.

In this regard, as an educator, I am recommending that, to complement 'social studies' done at the primary and secondary levels, a course about 'democracy, governance, and the roles and responsibilities of citizens' should be a part of the 'General Education' component of the undergraduate curricula of all tertiary level educational institutions in Jamaica, to develop informed and engaged citizens!

Access to Information Act (ATI)
The ATI was passed in 2002 and it gives members of the public the right to obtain information held by public authorities (government ministries, agencies, and

departments). "Every citizen," the ATI says, "shall have a right to obtain access to an official document, other than an exempt document.

Exempt documents are listed in Section III of the Act as those relating to matters such as Cabinet documents (some), law enforcement, legal privilege, international relations, national security, personal privacy, and the economy and trade secrets.

But, "the exemption of an official document or part thereof from disclosure shall not apply after the document has been in existence for 20 years, or such shorter period or longer period as the Minister may specify by order, subject to affirmative resolution." 'Information Officers' are deployed throughout the public sector and have the responsibility of facilitating requests made under the ATI Act.

The ATI is a critical tool that enables citizens to monitor and hold the government accountable, as well as being able to engage in informed dialogue concerning decisions that affect their lives. In a democracy, the right to know (RTK) by citizens is paramount.

Commenting on performing his duty as an active citizen when the ATI was being formulated, *Martin Henry* said "When I contributed my 'two pennies' to the development of the Access to Information Act, I kept making the point that in democratic government, with the rights and freedoms of citizens paramount, the business of government should be conducted in the town square. Access is the rule; secrecy the exception" [Source: The Gleaner, October 9, 2016].

Internationally, RTK Day began on September 28, 2002, in Sofia, Bulgaria at an international meeting of access to information advocates who proposed that a day be dedicated to the promotion of freedom of information worldwide. It is now celebrated globally and continues to grow and expand each year. Since that historic meeting in Sofia in 2002, 10 *Right to Know Principles* have been developed:

1. Access to information is a right of everyone.
2. Access is the rule - secrecy is the exception!
3. The right (of access) applies to all public bodies.
4. Making requests should be simple, speedy, and free.
5. Officials must assist requesters.
6. Refusals must be justified.
7. Public interest takes precedence over secrecy.
8. Everyone has the right to appeal an adverse decision.
9. Public bodies should proactively publish core information.
10. The right should be guaranteed by an independent body

My fellow Jamaicans, we must make maximum use of the ATI, using it as a powerful searchlight on how our governments and the public bureaucracy are operating and have operated.

This, however, is not the case now and needs to change because 'democracy dies in darkness' and good governance is predicated on transparency. It is the duty and responsibility of active Jamaican citizens to demand good governance by insisting on transparency and holding the government (of the day) accountable.

******

My Closing Argument

My fellow Jamaican, for Jamaica to function as a truly democratic society, we the people, the citizens, must be hypervigilant – distraction, like ignorance, is not bliss, and can even be dangerous.

Concerning our elected officials, we must always remember Lord John Acton's adage that "Power corrupts and absolute power corrupts absolutely." Yes, power can be intoxicating.

Therefore, we the people, must, by our actions, make it clear that we are the real bosses of Jamaica. We must not 'lef it up.'

The contemporary reality in Jamaica is 180° from what Vision 2030 envisages. Sadly, social and cultural pollutants, tribal politics, and poor governance have conspired to produce an awful alternative vision.

So, my fellow Jamaican, my *cri de coeur* (passionate appeal) is that we must rescue, realign, and reset our beloved country.

Now is the moment of choice and action to save our beloved country.

Now – the present - is the moment of choice and action.

Not tomorrow.

Not next week.

Not next month.

Not next year.

Now, my fellow Jamaican.

Now.

Future generations will be our judge. And what we do now, as active and engaged citizens, or the opposite, will determine their verdict on us.

The time now is 'rescue-Jamaica o'clock.'

****

About the Author

Dr. Paul W. Ivey is an activist academic, an active and engaged Jamaican citizen, a public affairs commentator, a historian, and the author of 18 books that are trellised upon robust research and solid scholarship. His books are crafted to animate and augment readers' minds and are available in e-book and paperback formats on the Internet.

****